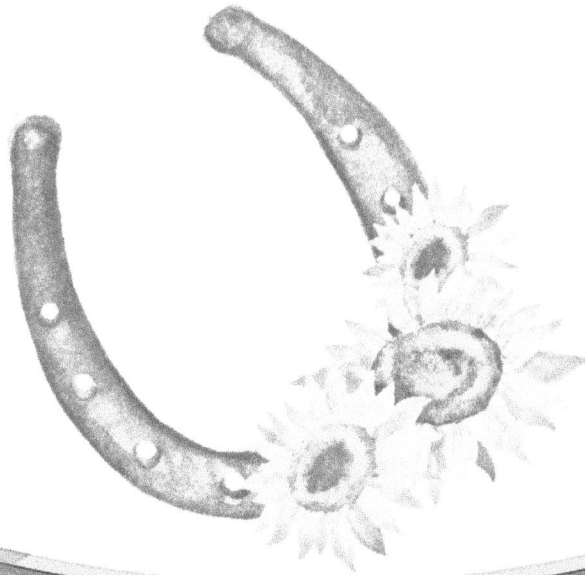

JAZZY HARMONY

Grayscale Coloring
WESTERN

I0135696

WANTED
DEAD OR ALIVE

100000$
· REWARD ·

TEXAS

★ OLD WEST ★

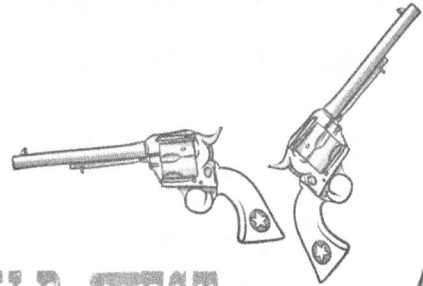

★ WILD WEST ★

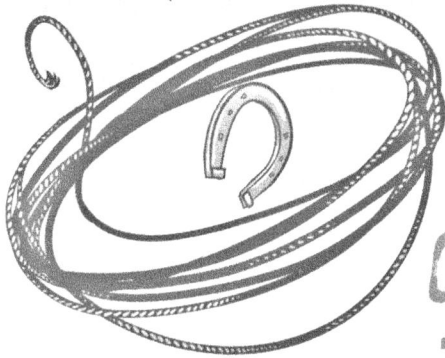

COWBOY

RODEO

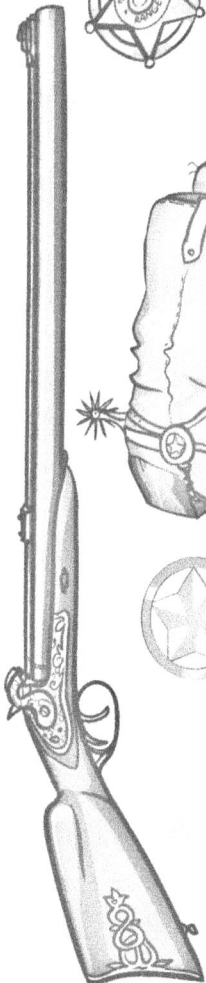

WILD WEST
COLLECTION

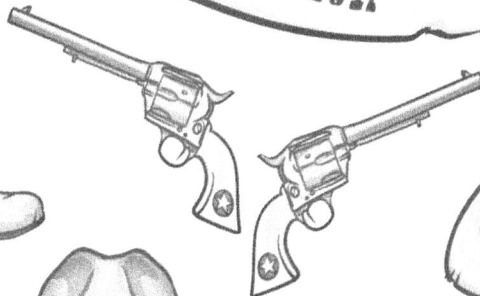

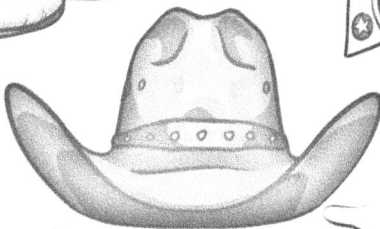

BIG ★
TEXAS

DON'T MESS
WITH
TEXAS

★ OLD WEST ★

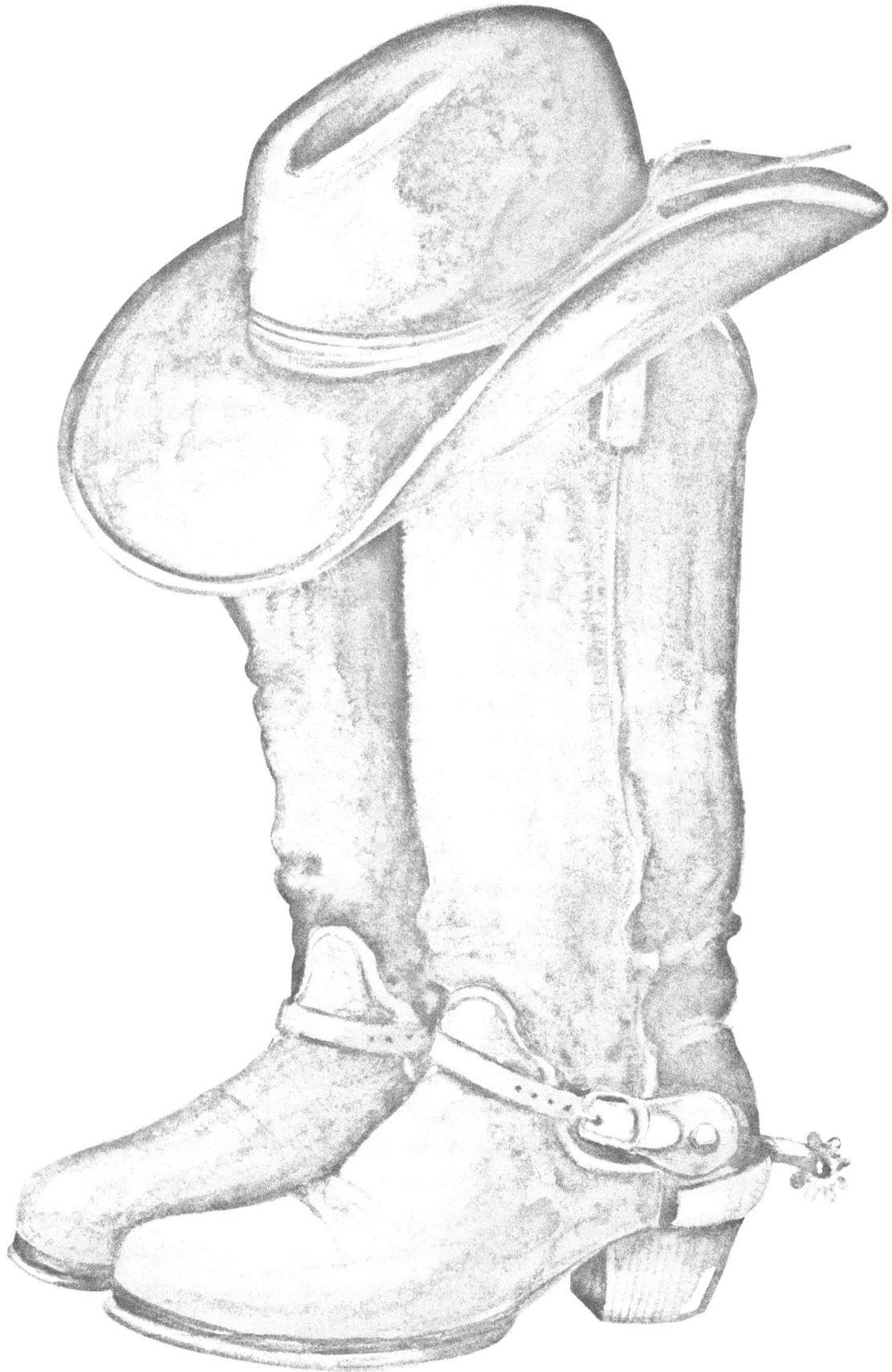

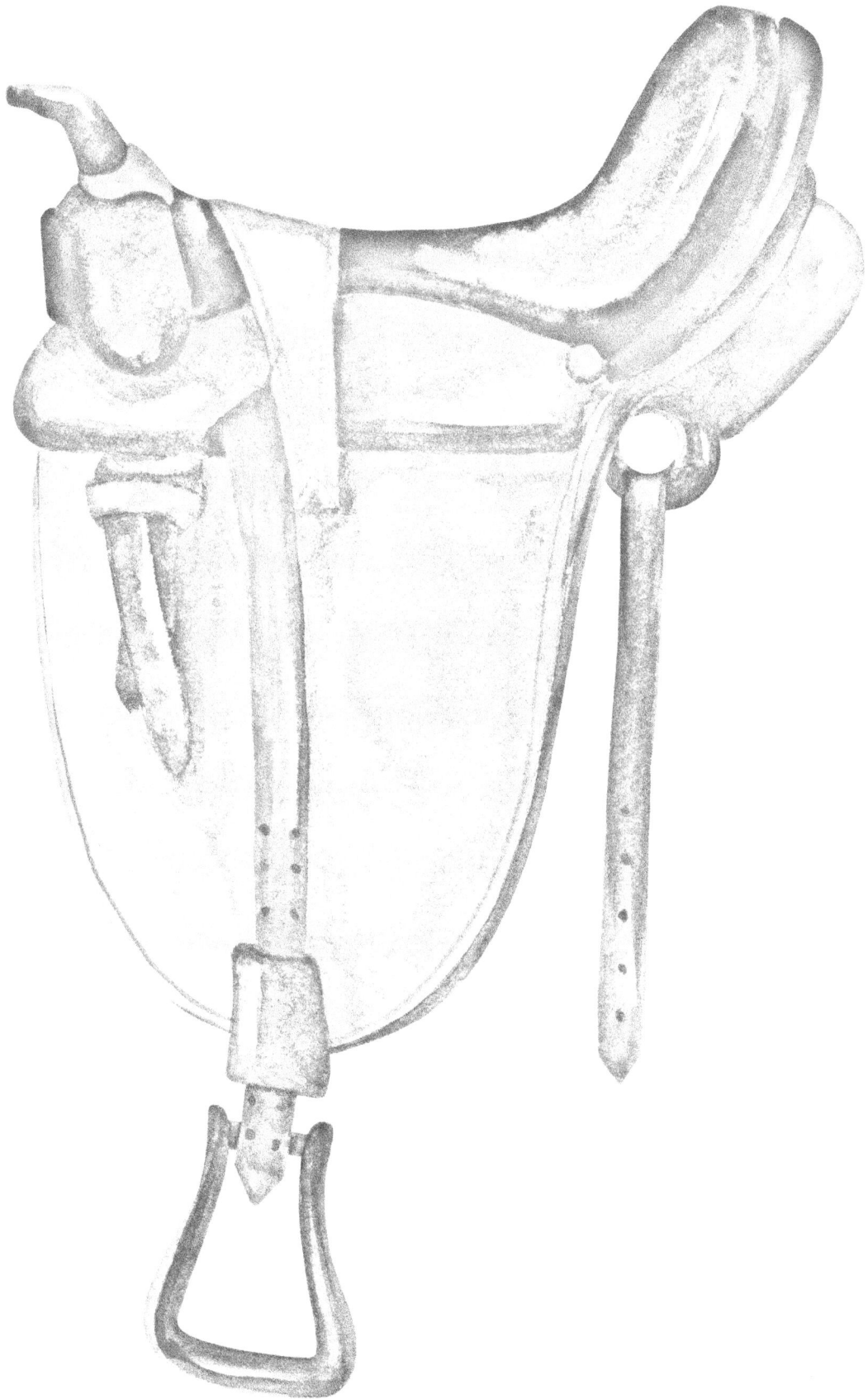

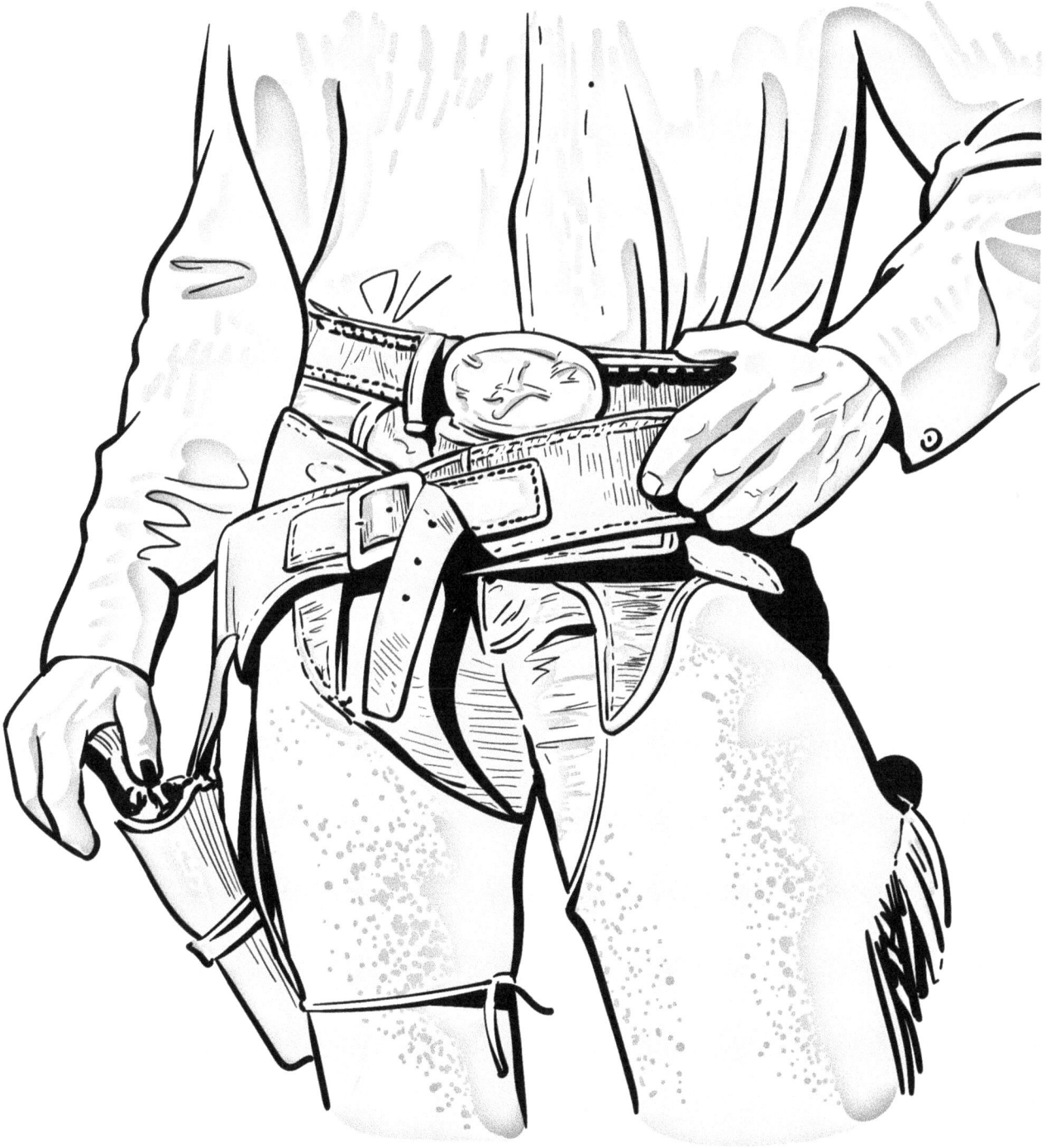

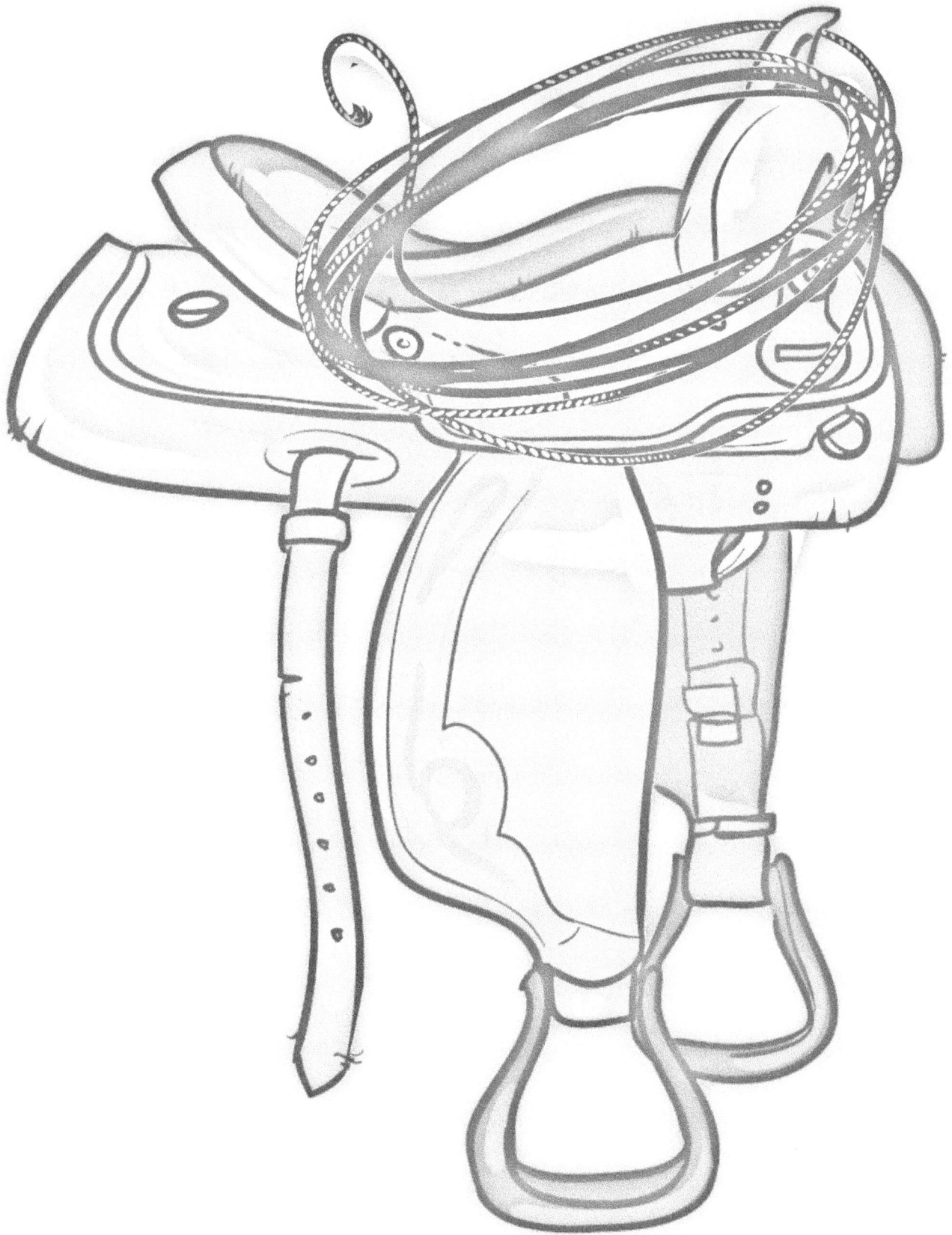

Cowgirl
spirit

WILD WEST
WELCOME

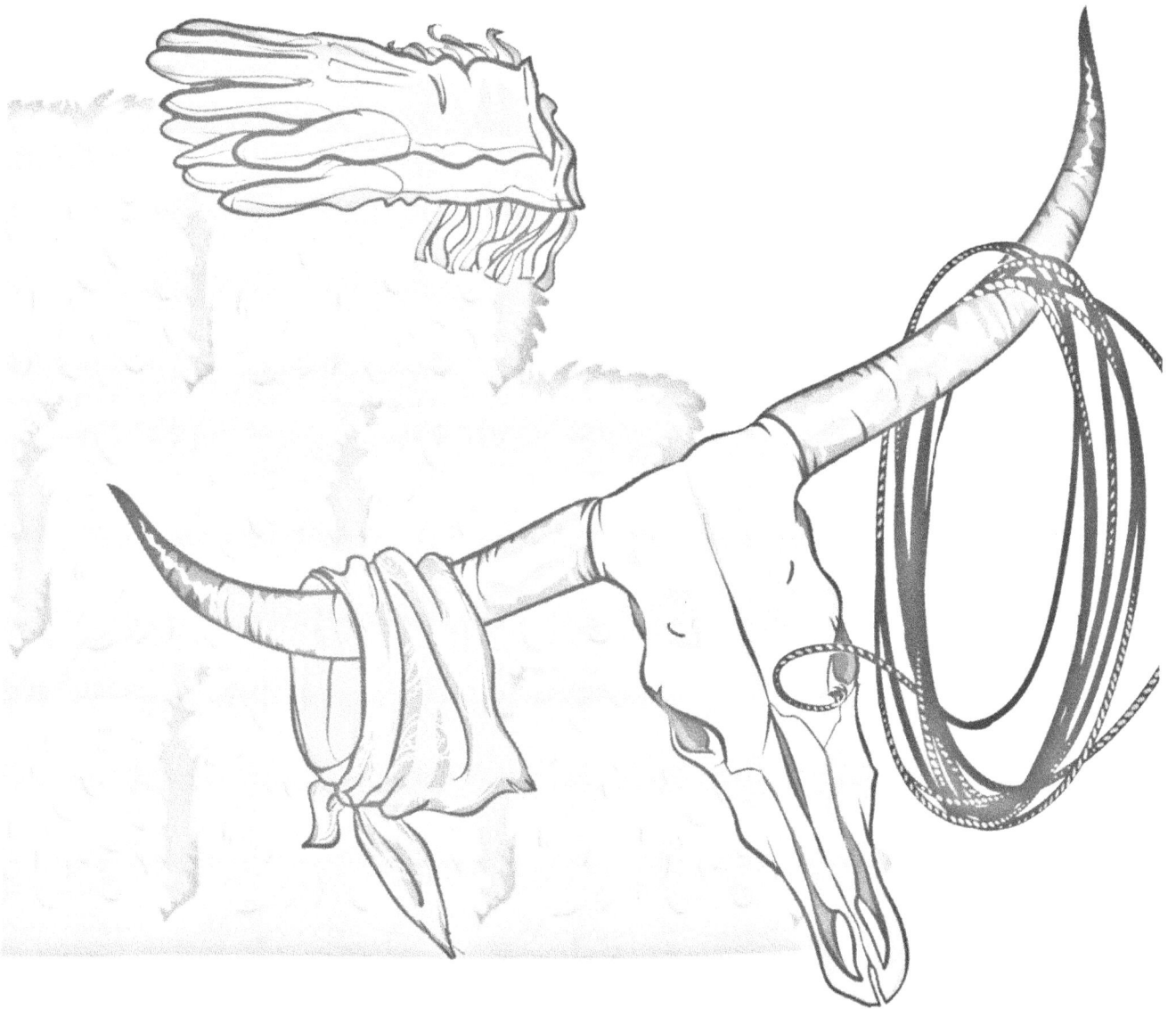

More coloring books by JAZZY HARMONY

Realistic

HORSE

grayscale animal coloring books for adults

JAZZY HARMONY

Coloring Books For Adults
DREAMCATCHER

Relaxing coloring book for adults

JAZZY HARMONY

FAMOUS CITY
Coloring Books For Adults
London

city escapes
coloring book

www.ingramcontent.com/pod-product-compliance
Lightning Source LLC
Chambersburg PA
CBHW080630030426
42336CB00018B/3143